This book belongs to:

....

MARVELLOUS HISTORY

How this collection works

This collection includes five amazing non-fiction texts that are ideal for encouraging your child's interest in history, from how travel has got faster, communication has got easier and how some incredible discoveries were made by mistake! These texts are packed full of fascinating information, with the same high-quality artwork and photos you would expect from any non-fiction book – but they are specially written so that your child can read them for themselves. They are carefully levelled and in line with your child's phonics learning at school.

It's very important for your child to have access to non-fiction as well as stories while they are learning to read. This helps them develop a wider range of reading skills, and prepares them for learning through reading. Most children love finding out about the world as they read – and some children prefer non-fiction to story books, so it's doubly important to make sure that they have opportunities to read both.

How to use this book

Reading should be a shared and enjoyable experience for both you and your child. Pick a time when your child is not distracted by other things, and when they are happy to concentrate for about 15 minutes. Choose just one of the non-fiction texts for each session, so that they don't get too tired. Read the tips on the next page, as they offer ideas and suggestions for getting the most out of this collection.

Tips for reading non-fiction

STEP 1

Before your child begins reading one of the non-fiction texts, look together at the contents page for that particular text. What does your child think the text will be about? Do they know anything about this subject already? Briefly talk about your child's ideas, and remind them of anything they know about the topic if necessary. Look at the page of notes and 'before reading' suggestions for each text, and use these to help introduce the text to your child.

STEP 2

Ask your child to show you some of the non-fiction features in the text – for example, the contents page, glossary and index, photos, labels and fact boxes. Can your child tell you how the contents page and index help you to find your way around the text? Point out that some tricky words are explained in the glossary.

STEP 3

Ask your child to read the text aloud. Encourage them to stop and look at the pictures, and talk about what they are reading either during the reading session, or afterwards. Your child will be able to read most of the words in the text, but if they struggle with a word, remind them to say the sounds in the word from left to right and then blend the sounds together to read the whole word, e.g. *v-a-m-p-ire, vampire*. If they have real difficulty, tell them the word and move on.

STEP 4

When your child has finished reading, talk about what they have found out. Which bits of the text did they like most, and why? Encourage your child to do some of the fun activities that follow each text.

CONTENTS

OXFORD
UNIVERSITY PRESS

Faster, Faster!

This text explores how transport has changed through time – and how it's got faster!

Before reading

What different ways of travelling has your child tried (e.g. walking, running, riding, car, bus, train, plane? Which was the fastest? Which is their favourite?

Look out for ...

… a boat with lots of oars

… a very old carving of a chariot

… a train that burned coal for power

… an aeroplane made from wood and cloth

… a vehicle that can travel into space!

FASTER, FASTER!

CONTENTS

Rob Alcraft

Feet were the first kind of transport. You can walk a long way, but it takes a long time. It would take nearly a year to walk around the world, and that's if you didn't stop at all.

But humans didn't stop at walking. Look below – over time we have invented faster and faster ways to travel.

First humans   Now

Long ago, running was the fastest way to travel.

It is hard work carrying things when you are walking.

What might be faster than walking or running?

Set Sail

Boats were the first way to go faster. People used paddles, or rowed their boats with oars. Later people added sails.

With sails, ships could use the wind to push them along. They could cross the sea and carry heavy **cargo**.

A very old painting of a boat from a tomb in Egypt.

Sails made ships faster.

Gallop

Long ago, people began to use animals for transport. Animals can carry heavy loads and they are faster than people. A horse can gallop much faster than a human can run.

Riding was a lot faster than walking!

A camel can carry the same load as the total amount six people can carry.

Yaks carry heavy loads.

Wheels are another very old invention. They are a good way to go faster.

Wheels make it easy to push or pull things along.

This is a very old stone carving showing a **chariot**.

This old bicycle has wooden wheels and metal tyres.

Steam trains were faster than anything before. Some trips took just hours instead of days.

Steam trains were powerful, too. One steam train was as strong as thousands of horses.

Steam trains burned coal for power.

A modern bullet train is many times faster than the first steam trains.

Vroom!

Cars made it easier to travel faster. They used new engines that burned **fuel**, such as **petrol**.

Now motor transport is everywhere. Lorries and vans carry **goods**, buses carry groups of people and lots of people own cars or motorbikes.

The first cars weren't that fast!

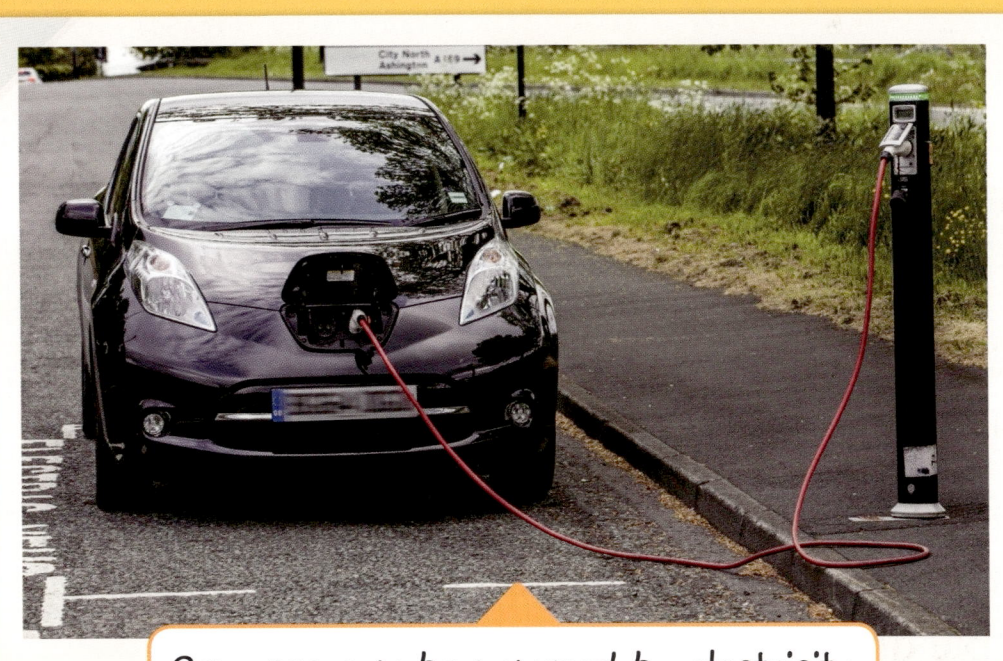

Cars can now be powered by electricity.

Fly

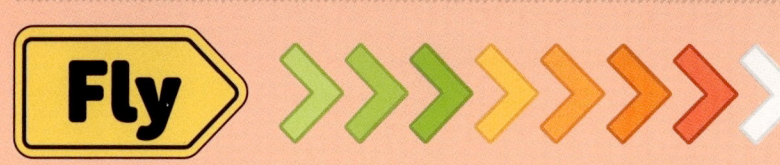

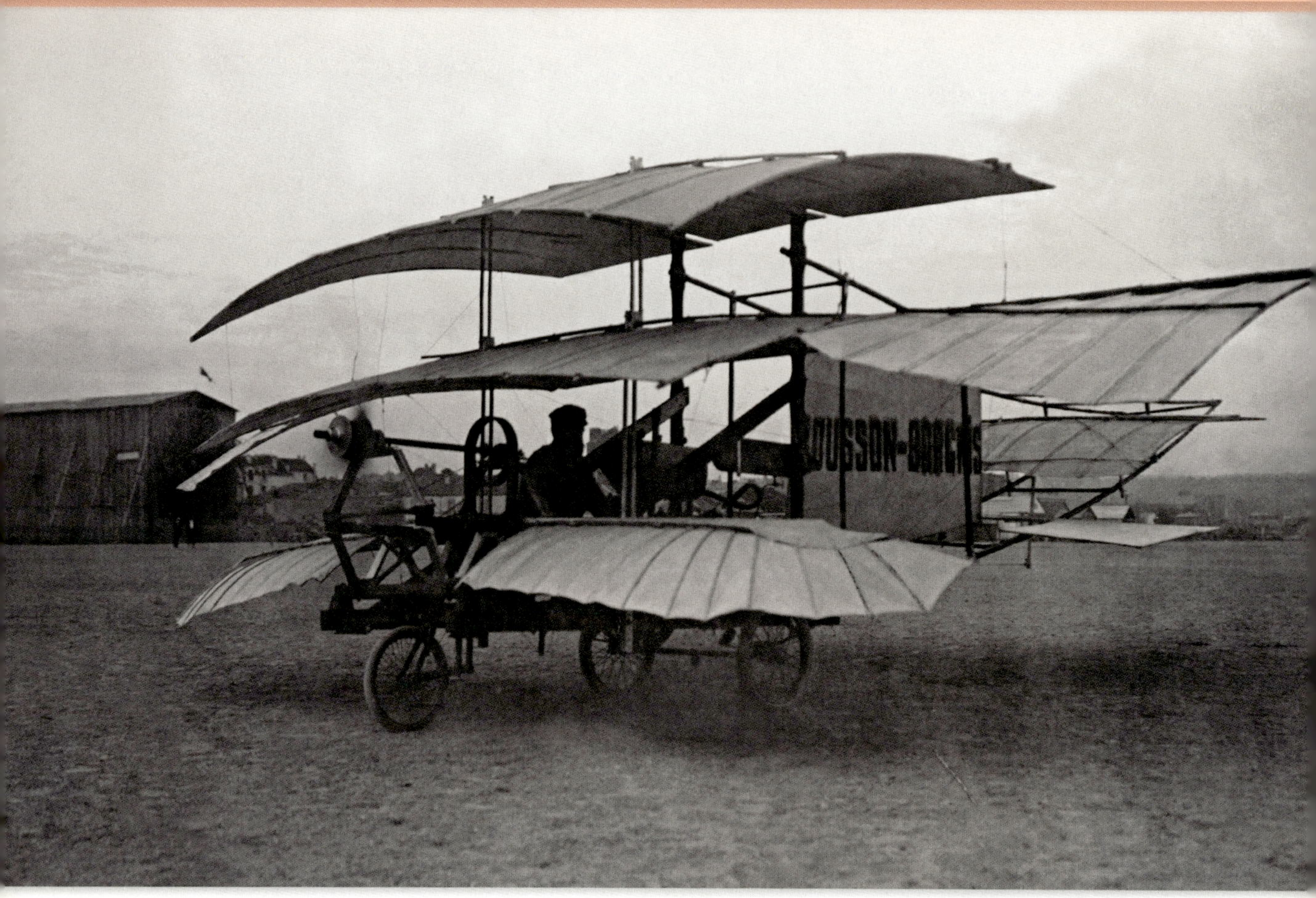

The first aircraft were unsafe and could not fly far.

Aircraft got safer and faster. Now passenger jets carry people and cargo all around the world.

The first aircraft were made from wood and cloth.

jet engine

Each of these jet engines is more powerful than a steam train.

Blast Off! >>>>>>>

Rockets can travel faster and further than anything before – even into space.

A space rocket travels over a thousand times faster than a human can run!

Space rockets need to carry lots of fuel. They have to be big!

Rocket engines blast out gas and flames.

Is Fastest Best?

What's the fastest way around the world? If a horse could gallop around the world without stopping, it would take about a month. It would take a space rocket less than two hours.

But not many of us have rockets! What's your favourite way to get around?

Glossary

cargo: goods carried in a ship or on an aircraft

chariot: a horse-drawn form of transport with two wheels

fuel: something that is burned to make power or heat

goods: things that people buy and sell

petrol: a liquid used as a fuel for engines

Index

Talk about it!

Do you think it's always best to travel as fast as possible?
Why, or why not?

Who is the fastest?

Number the pictures to show which is fastest.
Start with 1 for the slowest thing.

Edward Lear's Scrapbook

This text is a fascinating scrapbook full of information about the famous poet and artist, Edward Lear.

Before reading

Does your child already know anything about Edward Lear? For instance, they may know *The Jumblies* or one of his other poems. If not, flip through the text together to get a sense of who he was and when he lived.

Look out for ...

… a beautiful parrot picture

… a drawing by Queen Victoria

… a picture of Edward Lear with wings

… a man with a beard full of birds

… an owl and a pussy-cat

EDWARD LEAR'S SCRAPBOOK

CONTENTS

Edward Lear was an artist and a poet. He lived from 1812 to 1888.

Michaela Morgan

When I Was Little

My name is Edward Lear. I was born in London, England, in 1812.

I had lots of brothers and sisters. I was one of the youngest.

My family didn't have enough money. When I was four years old, I was sent away from home. I went to live with my big sister, Ann.

Ann

Ann looked after me. I needed a lot of looking after because I was ill so much.

I had sniffs and sneezes. I had coughs and wheezes. I had shivers and shakes and gloominess. I often felt sad.

Me!

My Paintings

I loved drawing. I started to make money from my art when I was 15 years old.

I liked to draw pictures of birds.

I **published** my first book in 1830, when I was 17 years old.

It was filled with pictures of parrots.

MACROCERCUS ARARAUNA.

Blue & Yellow Maccaw

Later, I even gave drawing lessons to **Queen Victoria**.

One of Queen Victoria's drawings

My Travels

I wanted to find out more about birds and different places.

So I went travelling.

lovely

very hot

sandy

R LONDON 3739
No. 43

The Crimson Bird.

The Light=Green Bird.

Post Card

for correspondence · for address only

domestic
one pence
foreign
three pence

I made up funny poems and pictures and put them in my letters. My friends liked them!

A postcard to a friend

beautiful birds

marvellous mountains

very hot

My Poems

In 1846, I **published** my first book of poems. It was called *A Book of Nonsense*.

There were 72 poems in it!

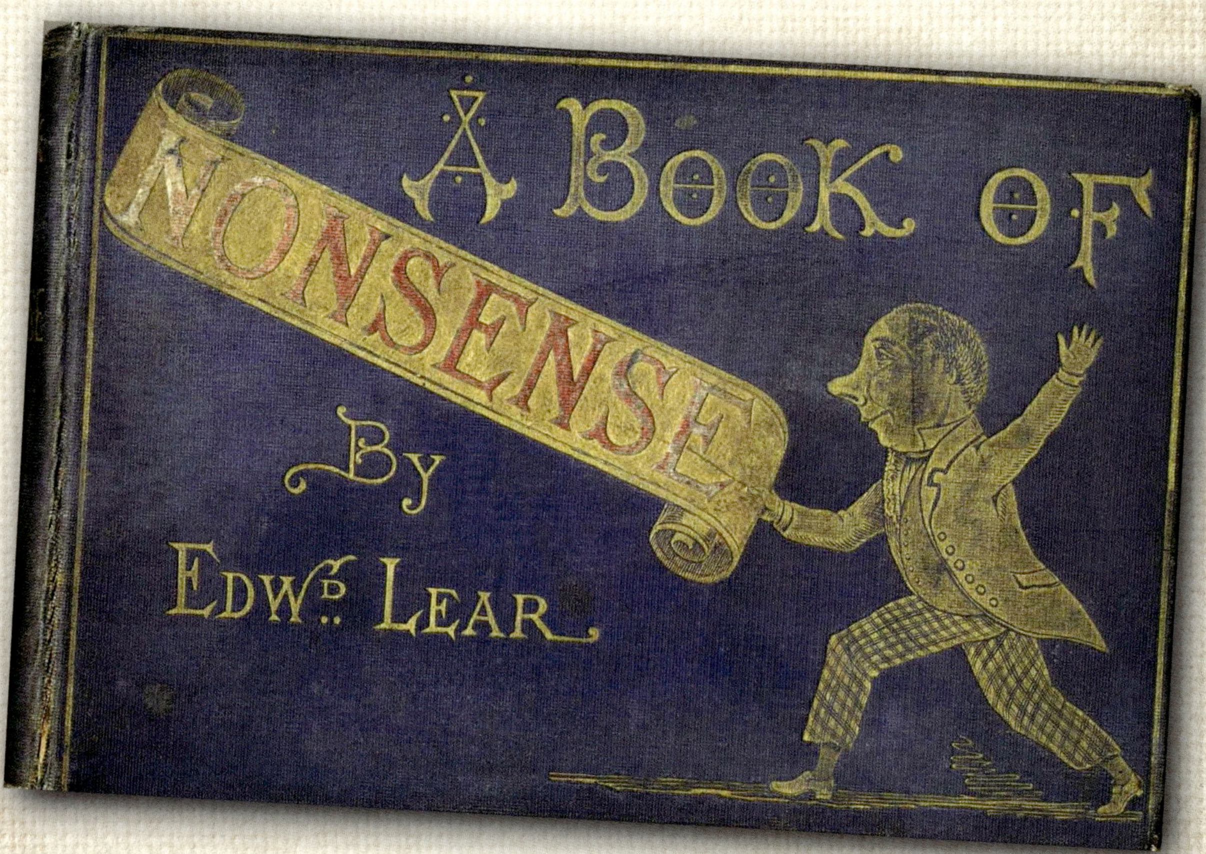

I wrote many short, funny poems. I called them 'nonsenses'. Other people called them **limericks**. Here's one:

There was an Old Man with a beard,
Who said, "It is just as I feared!
Two Owls and a Hen,
Four Larks and a Wren,
Have all built their nests in my beard!"

There was an Old Man with a beard, who said, "It is just as I feared!—
Two Owls and a Hen, four Larks and a Wren,
Have all built their nests in my beard!"

My Characters

The Owl and the Pussy-cat

When I was working, I dreamed a bit ...
I doodled a bit ... I let my mind wander.
I made up strange characters and gave them
wonderful names – like Jumblies and Pobble
and Dong. Then I sent them on adventures.

the Jumblies

the Pobble

the Dong

I had fun drawing and writing. I worked hard so that I could earn money to buy food. My favourite things to eat were bread and cheese.

When I Was Old

When I was old, I wanted to live in the sun. I moved to Italy with my cat, Foss.

Foss grew old and one day, she died. It was sad but she had lived a good life. I gave her a big **funeral**.

Edward Lear died in January 1888.

People still enjoy his books and poems today. Try reading *The Owl and the Pussy-cat*, his most famous poem.

The Owl and the Pussy-cat went to sea
In a beautiful pea-green boat,
They took some honey, and plenty of money
Wrapped up in a five pound note.

Glossary

funeral: a ceremony for someone who has died

limericks: funny poems with five lines

published: when a book is printed and ready for everyone to read

Queen Victoria: the British queen from 1837 to 1901

Some of Edward Lear's poems that you might like:

- *The Dong with the Luminous Nose*

- *The Jumblies*

- *The Owl and the Pussy-cat*

- *The Quangle Wangle's Hat*

- *The Pobble Who Has No Toes*

Talk about it!

Which of Edward Lear's pictures or poems did you like best? Why?

Edward Lear word search

Can you find the 8 words?

a	l	i	m	e	r	i	c	k	e
n	q	p	w	j	h	f	o	s	s
o	n	o	d	u	k	x	p	r	i
n	j	b	f	m	t	y	a	m	l
s	r	b	e	b	o	i	r	s	z
e	u	l	h	l	c	e	r	b	v
n	b	e	r	i	p	q	o	w	l
s	f	l	e	e	b	g	t	h	o
e	h	p	u	s	s	y	c	a	t

Jumblies

owl

pussy-cat

Foss

Pobble

limerick

nonsense

parrot

History's Marvellous Mistakes

This text explores three amazing discoveries that were made by mistake!

Before reading

Does your child think mistakes are usually marvellous? Talk about the idea that sometimes, good things happen by accident.

> ## Look out for ...
>
> ... an *enormous* bowl of cereal
>
> ... an explorer who used to sell cheese
>
> ... a city discovered by accident
>
> ... some accidental biscuits
>
> ... a mouldy experiment

HISTORY'S MARVELLOUS MISTAKES

CONTENTS

Ciaran Murtagh

Marvellous Mistakes

Everybody makes mistakes! I do. Once I made my dad sneeze off his moustache!

But mistakes aren't always bad. Some brilliant things were only discovered by mistake.

Let's meet the people behind three of history's most marvellous mistakes!

The explorer **Christopher Columbus** found a new **continent**, which he wasn't even looking for!

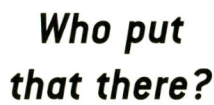

Who put that there?

The healthy **Kellogg brothers** invented breakfast cereal by accident!

Shh! I'm working!

And **Dr Alexander Fleming** invented a new medicine by going on holiday!

Christopher Columbus

Christopher Columbus, 1451–1506

Christopher Columbus was born in 1451. People think he first went to sea when he was ten. Before that, people say he helped his father sell cheese.

Bye, Dad!

CHEESE

At sea, Columbus learned different languages. He learned about **tides** and how to find his way using the stars. By 1492, he was ready to make his marvellous mistake!

In Columbus's time, people could sail from Europe to Asia, but the **route** was dangerous.

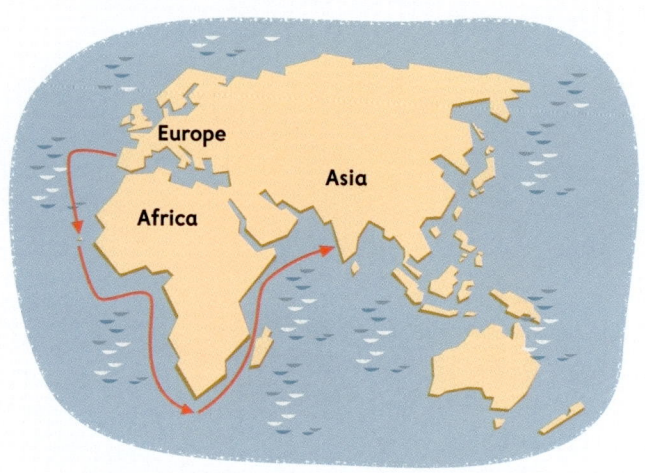

Columbus thought he could find a quicker and safer route by heading west. In 1492, he set sail to prove it. No one knew there was a continent in the way.

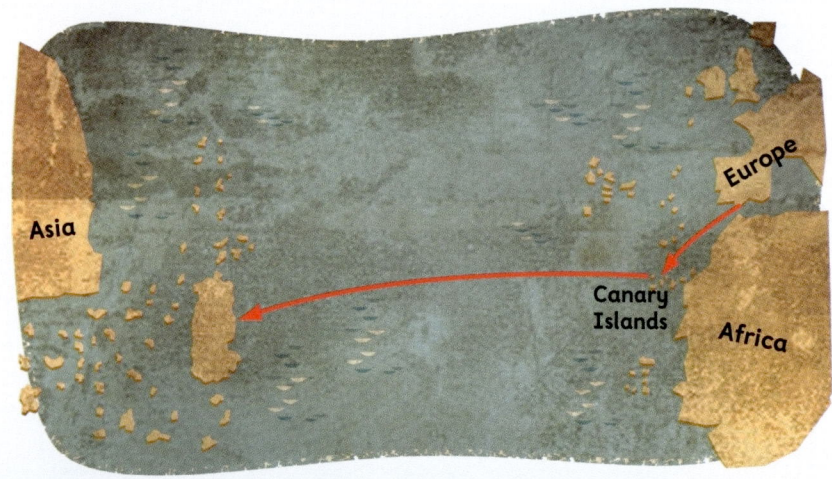

Columbus's planned route

The journey took ten weeks.

Are we nearly there yet?

Columbus thought he had arrived in Asia. But actually, he had found the continent of America!

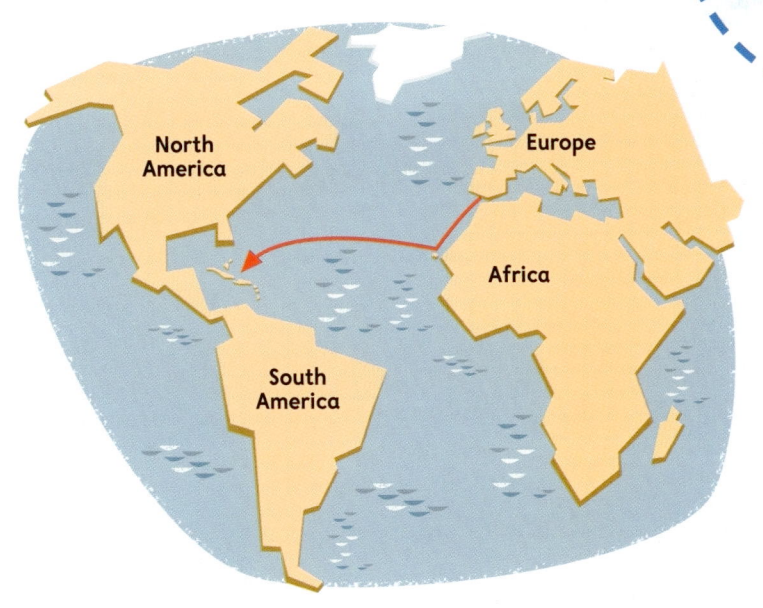

Columbus's actual route

Columbus stayed and explored.

Then he went back
and told everyone
about what he
called 'Western Asia'.
The discovery made
him rich.

Columbus died in 1506, still convinced that the land he had found was part of Asia.

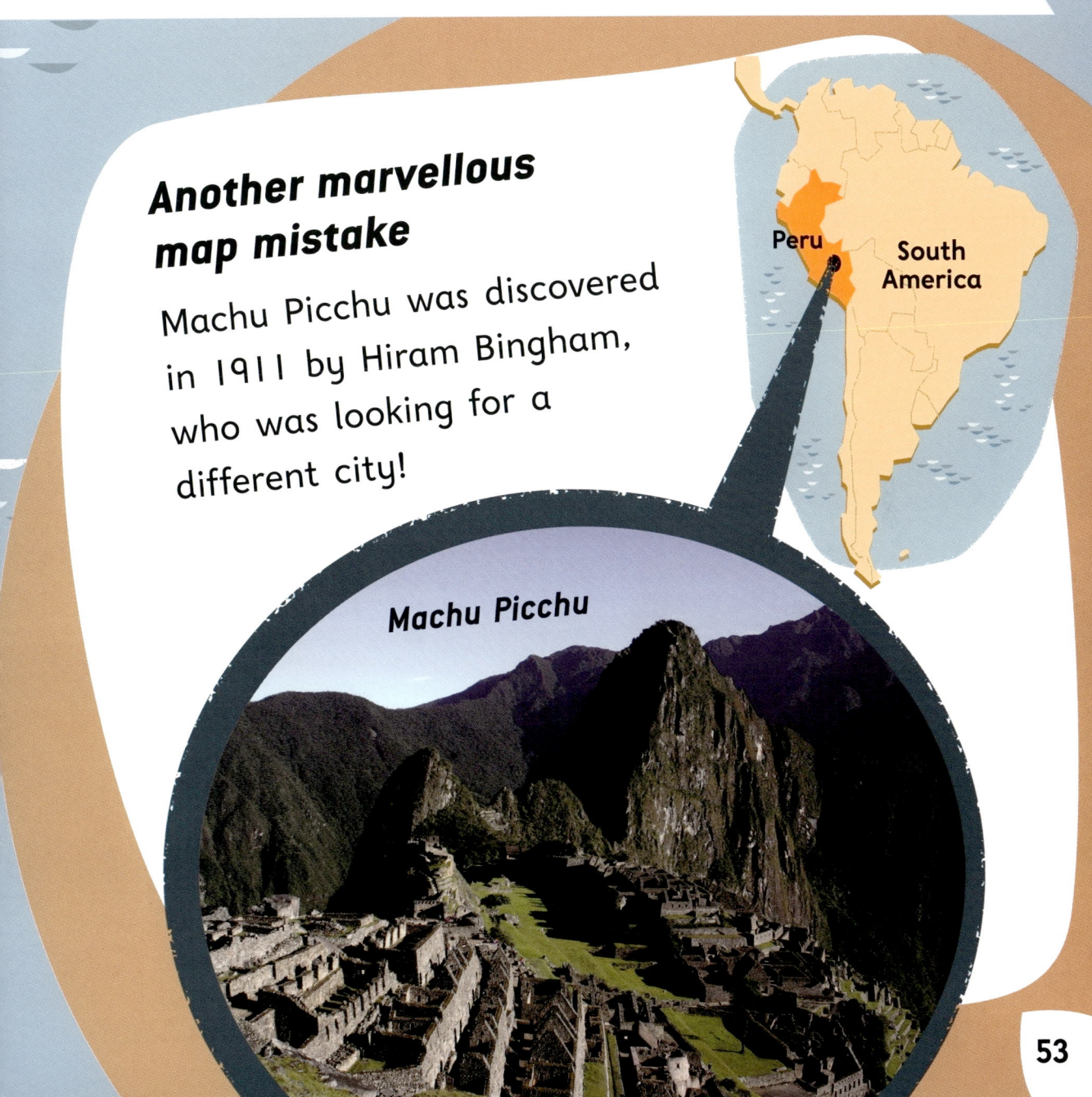

Another marvellous map mistake

Machu Picchu was discovered in 1911 by Hiram Bingham, who was looking for a different city!

Peru

South America

Machu Picchu

The Kellogg Brothers

Will Kellogg, 1860–1951

John and *Will Kellogg* were two American brothers, born in the mid-1800s.

John was a doctor. He and Will ran a **health resort** where they taught other people about healthy food and exercise.

John Kellogg, 1852–1943

In the 1890s, breakfast wasn't always a very healthy meal.

John and Will decided to invent a new, healthier breakfast. On 8th August 1894, they made their marvellous mistake.

The brothers were cooking wheat to make healthy bread. Then they were called away.

When they came back, the wheat had gone **stale**.

They made flakes out of the stale wheat.

John and Will toasted the flakes. They tasted good! The brothers tried out different **grains** and found that flakes made with corn tasted best.

Serious cereal statistic

The world's largest bowl of cereal held 1000 kilograms of cornflakes.

In 1906, the brothers argued. Will wanted to add sugar to the recipe. John did not.

Will set up his own cornflake factory and called it Kellogg's.

It's still going today. The two brothers never spoke to each other again.

Another marvellous munchable mistake

Chocolate chip cookies were invented in 1911 by Ruth Graves Wakefield while she was trying to make chocolate-flavoured cookies.

Alexander Fleming

Alexander Fleming was born in Scotland in 1881. He was a doctor who studied bacteria. Bacteria are tiny bugs that are too small to be seen. Some bacteria can cause diseases.

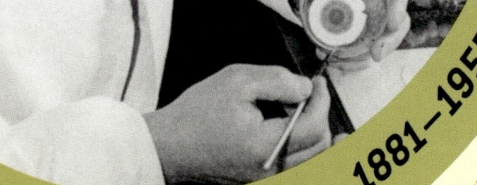

Alexander Fleming, 1881–1955

In the First World War, Fleming worked as a doctor. He noticed that many soldiers died because harmful bacteria **infected** their wounds.

He started looking for a cure.
This led to his marvellous mistake.

In 1928, Fleming was working on bacteria experiments. He went on holiday. When he got back, some of his experiments were covered in mould.

Some of the mould had killed the harmful bacteria. It was the cure Fleming had been looking for! He called his discovery 'mould juice' – but he soon changed the name to penicillin (*say* pen-i-sil-in).

Would you like some mould juice?

Fleming couldn't find a way to turn his discovery into medicine. But other scientists continued his work. In 1941, they started treating people with their new medicine – the first antibiotics (*say* an-tee-bigh-o-tiks).

Another marvellous medical mistake

X-rays were discovered in 1895 by Wilhelm Röntgen, who was studying something else.

Spooky!

Antibiotics have saved millions of lives. Fleming's **laboratory** is now a museum.

So don't worry if you get lost, burn your toast or forget to tidy your room! Your mistake might just change the world!

It's not messy! I'm experimenting!

Glossary

continent: one of the world's main large areas of land

grains: cereal crops used as food, like wheat, rice, barley or corn

health resort: a place you can visit to learn to be more healthy

infected: filled with disease

laboratory: a room where you can do scientific experiments

route: the way to get from one place to another

stale: dry and no longer good to eat

tides: movements of the sea, caused by the moon

Index

Talk about it!

Where was I trying to get to when I accidentally found America?

Marvellous mistakes

Complete the crossword.

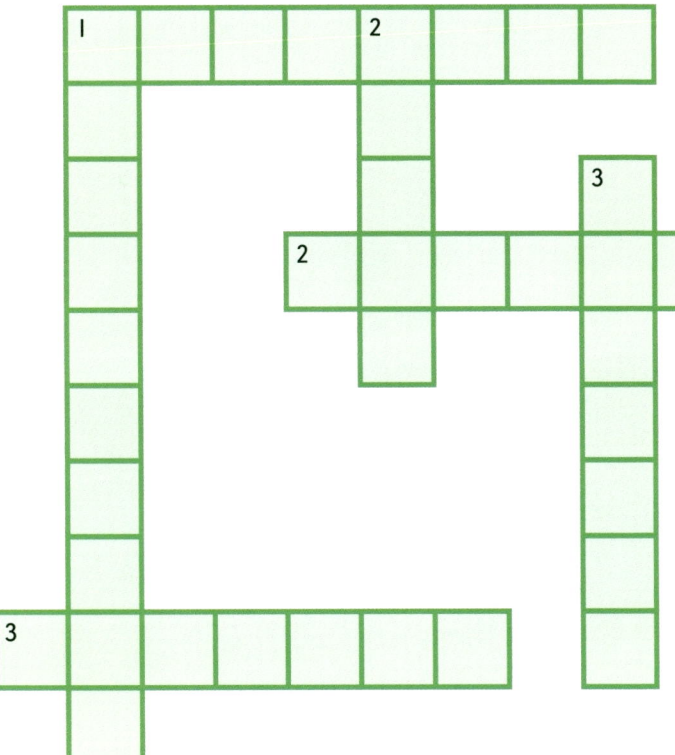

Across

1. He found America by mistake.
2. He discovered penicillin.
3. The surname of the inventors of cornflakes.

Down

1. A crunchy breakfast cereal invented by mistake.
2. This grew on an experiment.
3. A lot of things in this text happened by m_____.

Smoke Signals to Smartphones

This text explores how ways of communicating have changed through history.

Before reading

Ask your child how many ways of sending messages they can think of. How do they think people sent messages long ago?

Look out for ...

... paintings that send messages

... the way messages were sent on the Great Wall of China

... some helpful pigeons

... the word 'hello' spelled out with flags

... a machine that sends coded messages

SMOKE SIGNALS TO SMARTPHONES

CONTENTS

Becca Heddle

We Like To Talk!

Talking has been important to people for thousands of years.
And when we are apart, we find ways to stay in touch.

All through history, people have used the latest technology to send messages – from cave paintings to signals through space. We keep finding faster and better ways of communicating.

Messages From Prehistory

About 20,000 years ago, people did not know how to write. But these **prehistoric** people made paintings on cave walls. We can still see their messages today.

Messages In Smoke

About 2800 years ago, people were sending
smoke signals along the **Great Wall of China**.
People watched from towers and passed on the messages.
They copied the signals they saw.

We can send messages hundreds of miles in a day!

But it doesn't work when it's windy or rainy.

People still use smoke signals to call for help.

75

Pigeon Post

Pigeons can find their way home from anywhere. Around 3000 years ago, people started sending messages using pigeons.

This pigeon from World War I carried its message in here.

Dispatch Riders

In **Persia** around 2600 years ago, horse riders carried messages. Each rider passed the message on, until it reached the right person.

Pony Express riders delivered messages across America in the 1860s.

79

Postal Systems

By the 1600s, many more people could read and write. Some countries set up postal systems, which anyone could use.

Mail coaches carried letters between post offices.

People had to pay for every sheet of paper they posted.

I'm writing in two different directions, so I only have to send one page!

By 1830, trains were taking letters hundreds of miles in a day.

Flagging It Up

H E L L O

Around 250 years ago in France, people invented semaphore (*say* sem-a-for). It used wooden arms on towers, with positions for different words. Soon, British ships were using semaphore to send messages with flags.

83

Morse Code

In the 1830s, Morse code was invented. Morse code messages were long and short signals. They went along an electrical wire. Someone decoded the message at the other end.

message in Morse code

Telephones

early telephone

1950s telephone

The telephone was invented in 1876. Now you could actually speak to someone who was miles away. Your voices went along the wire.

Mobile Phones

In 1973, a 'mobile' phone was invented – it didn't need a wire. By 2013, more people had a mobile phone than a toilet!

Mobile phones mean people can make calls to and from almost anywhere in the world – even in places with no wires at all.

Computers

In the 1950s, computers were enormous. They took up whole rooms. They got smaller and by the 1990s, many people had a computer at home.

Smartphones

an early
smartphone

Smartphones started to become popular in 2007.
A single smartphone is more powerful than all
of the computers that helped to land the
first man on the Moon.

93

What Next?

Human communications have come a long way, from cave paintings to email. What might come next? Will we be able to send computer messages straight to each other's brains?

We have sent spacecraft out into the universe. They carry messages in case someone out there might read them. Perhaps one day we will get a message from the stars!

Glossary

Great Wall of China: a very long wall in China, built to keep invaders out

Persia: a large ancient kingdom, more or less where Iran is now

prehistoric: from a very long time ago, before written records were kept

Index

Talk about it!

Which do you think would be the best way to send a secret message? Why?

Communication word search

Can you find the communication words?

r	p	a	i	n	t	i	n	g	s
a	s	h	c	p	s	m	o	k	e
m	y	d	o	i	k	w	j	p	m
o	u	s	m	g	t	i	b	n	a
r	h	e	p	e	i	o	u	f	p
s	b	n	u	o	r	v	l	k	h
e	q	z	t	n	l	d	c	i	o
h	c	y	e	a	x	v	j	e	r
s	m	a	r	t	p	h	o	n	e

Morse

semaphore

smartphone

computer

smoke

pigeon

painting

Meet a Genius

This text talks about three amazing geniuses of music, science and maths: Wolfgang Mozart, Marie Curie and Srinivasa Ramanujan.

Before reading

Has your child heard of any of the people in this text? If not, briefly flip through together to find out a bit about them, before your child starts reading.

Look out for ...

... a musical child star

... a dish of dumplings

... a strange ear

... a dog called Lancet

... a man who was friends with numbers

MEET A GENIUS

CONTENTS

Rob Alcraft

A genius is a person with an amazing ability. They can do things that other people can't do.

Come and find out about three geniuses.

Which genius wore her wedding dress to work?

Which genius failed most of his exams?

Which genius was scared of trumpets?

The Wonder Child

Wolfgang Amadeus Mozart
(*say* wolf-gang am-a-day-us moat-sart)

Mozart was a musical genius.

He began to **compose** music at the age of five.

- Born 1756, in Austria

- Composed over 600 pieces of music

- Died aged 35

Mozart was a child star. He travelled with his sister and father, and played concerts for kings and queens.

sister · Mozart · father · harpsichord

Mozart could play the **harpsichord** from the age of four.

Mozart never went to school –
his dad taught him at home.

He wrote his first **symphony**
when he was eight.

When Mozart gave concerts,
he wore fashionable white wigs.

Mozart loved:
dumplings,
his wife Constanze –
and his hair too!

Liver dumplings were his favourite food.

He married Constanze in 1782.

He had his hair styled every day.

And he loved me!

Mozart taught his pet bird to sing some of his music.

Mozart hated:

trumpets,
Paris –
and being told what to do!

He was afraid of trumpets – they made him cry!

Mozart hated being told what to do. He argued so much that he once lost his job!

He thought that Paris was dirty.

Mozart thought that he and his son had weird ears. He made this drawing to prove it!

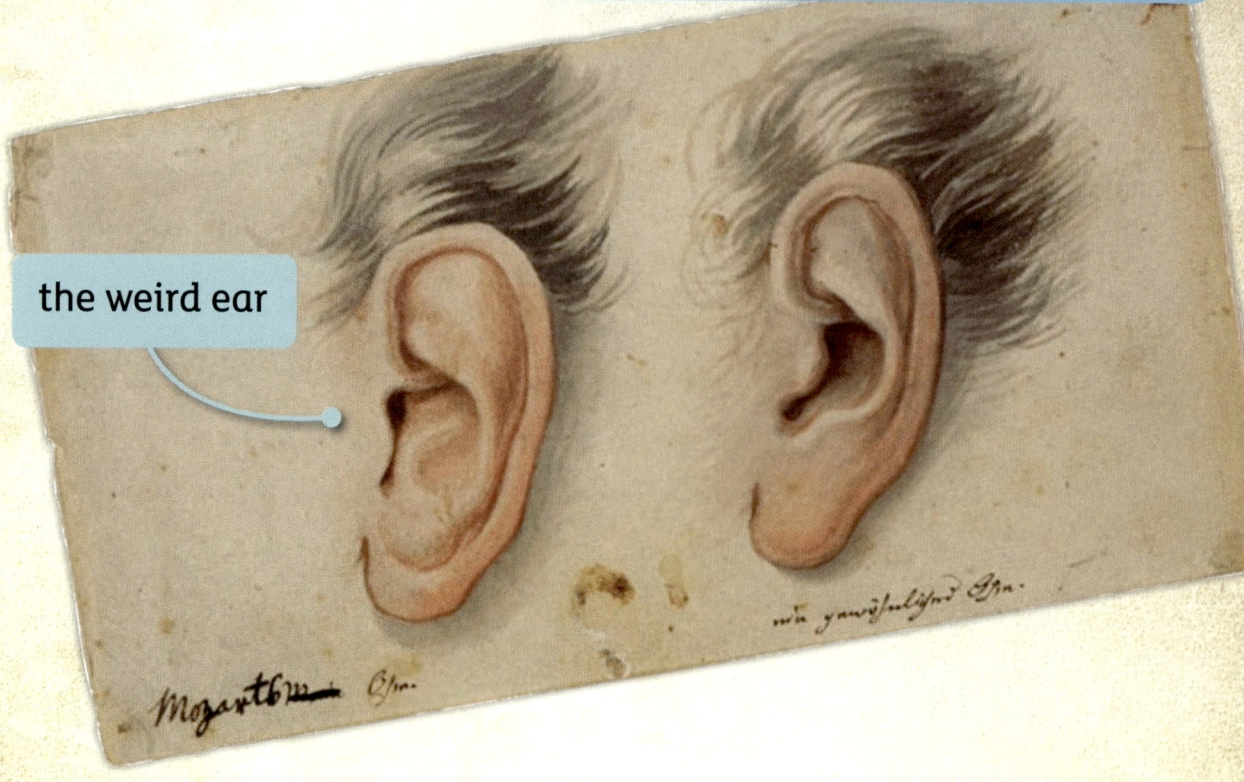

the weird ear

Mozart composed music in his head. He said he thought about music all day long.

He had to travel for work a lot.
Mozart spent 3720 days on the road.
That's over 10 years of travel!

Genius!

Mozart is one of the most famous composers ever.

Every year thousands of people come to Mozart's home town for a festival of his music.

Greatest Work

The Magic Flute is an **opera** by Mozart. It's still performed over 500 times a year around the world!

The Woman Who Changed Science

Marie Curie
(*say* ma-ree cure-ee)

Curie was a science genius.

Her discoveries about **radiation** changed science for ever.

- Born 1867, in Poland

- Won two **Nobel Prizes** for her discoveries in science

- Died aged 66

She taught herself to read aged four.

Curie

sisters

father

Her dad was a science teacher.

Curie was good at school, but girls weren't allowed to go to university in Poland at that time.

Instead, Curie studied in secret classes.

She worked for seven years as a **governess**. When Curie had saved enough money, she went to study at a university in France.

Curie loved:
books,
hot chocolate –
and Pierre!

bonjour hello
здравствуйте guten Tag
cześć

She read books in five languages.

When she was a student she survived on hot chocolate, bread and fruit.

She loved me too!

Her dog, Lancet, was big and badly behaved.

She married Pierre in 1895. He was a scientist too.

Curie hated:

learning Russian history,
being a governess –
and not sharing!

She didn't like learning Russian history.

She only worked as a governess so she could save money to study.

She preferred to share her science ideas, rather than make money from them.

When Marie and Pierre got married, they were poor.

They had to work in a leaky shed and Curie wore her old wedding dress for work!

Curie worked hard for a long time to find out about radiation.
She discovered a new metal called radium.

The metal gave off a strange energy that Curie called radioactivity.

After dark the Curies' shed was filled with a blue-green glow. The glow came from radiation.

Danger

Curie's notebooks are so radioactive that it is dangerous to touch them.

Genius!

Curie was the first person ever to win two Nobel Prizes for science.

At the time, some people thought women should not work in science. Marie Curie showed that women could be scientists. She led the way for other women to study science.

Greatest Work

Curie's work proved it was possible to split an **atom**.

The Man Who Dreamed of Numbers

Srinivasa Ramanujan
(*say* sree-nee-va-sa ra-man-oo-jan)

Ramanujan was a maths genius.

He said that sometimes he got the answers to maths puzzles in his dreams.

- Born 1887, in India

- Taught himself maths and thought up thousands of new maths ideas

- Died aged 32

mother

Ramanujan

Ramanujan loved maths – but he wouldn't study anything else.

He failed all his college exams – except maths of course!

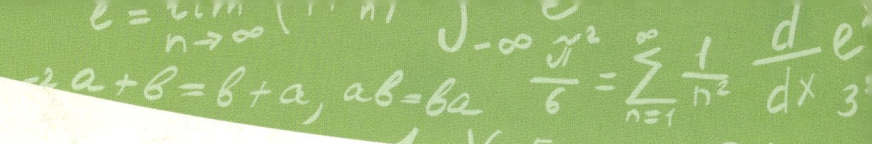

Ramanujan worked
outside his house.

Ramanujan invented his
own maths language to write
down his ideas.

He started out writing on
a slate using chalk.

Ramanujan loved:

notebooks,
numbers –
and talking!

He filled notebooks with maths answers.

Someone who knew him wrote that every number was his friend.

A friend once had to throw a pot of water over his head to stop him talking!

He loved me too!

When he lived in England, Ramanujan asked his family to send him coconut oil.

Ramanujan hated:

leaving his home in India,
English shoes –
and English weather!

When he was first asked to come to England, Ramanujan didn't want to go.

He didn't like English shoes, so he wore slippers instead – even outside!

The English weather made him miserable.

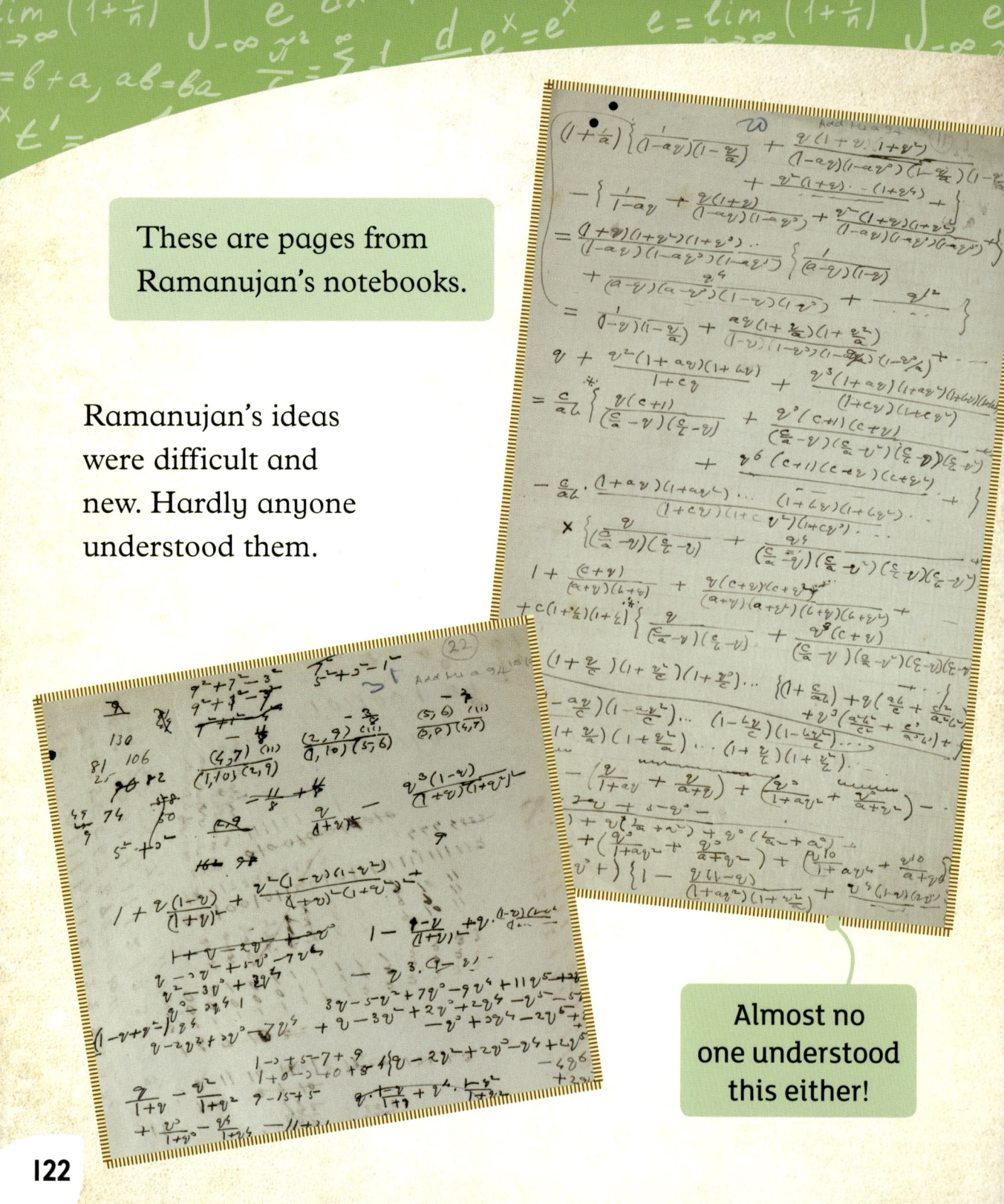

These are pages from Ramanujan's notebooks.

Ramanujan's ideas were difficult and new. Hardly anyone understood them.

Almost no one understood this either!

Ramanujan worked at Cambridge University. He missed home, but he still came up with amazing new maths ideas.

At home, Ramanujan dressed in Indian clothes. When he went to England he wore a suit for the first time.

He went punting.

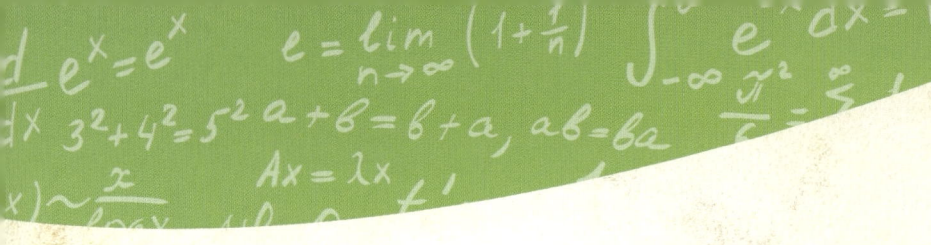

Today, Ramanujan's maths is helping scientists to work out what happens inside a **black hole** – mind-boggling!

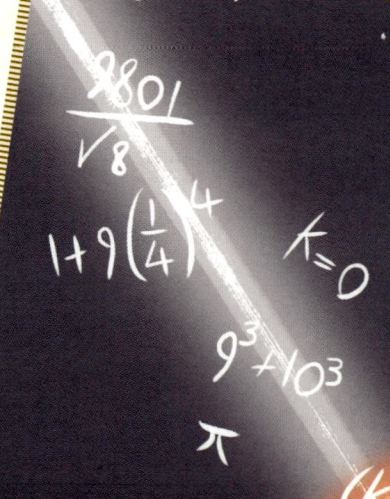

Greatest Work

Websites use number patterns which Ramanujan worked out.

Being a Genius Is Simple!

You've met three geniuses, so now you know their simple secrets:

- they all had amazing ability;
- they all loved their work;
- they all worked really hard, and never stopped.

Glossary

atom: tiny parts from which everything is made

black hole: a part of space that pulls light and things into it

compose: to make up or create

governess: a woman who teaches children in their home

harpsichord: a musical instrument like a small piano

Nobel Prizes: prizes awarded for amazing work in science, medicine, and other subjects

opera: a play where all the words are sung

radiation: a dangerous type of energy which comes from some materials like radium

symphony: a long piece of music played by lots of musicians together

Index

Talk about it!

Whose dog was I?
What was my owner
famous for?

Whose is whose?

Match the objects with their owners!

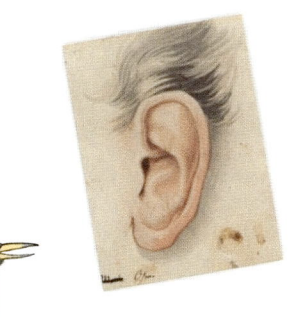

OXFORD
UNIVERSITY PRESS

Great Clarendon Street, Oxford, OX2 6DP, United Kingdom

Oxford University Press is a department of the University of Oxford. It furthers the University's objective of excellence in research, scholarship, and education by publishing worldwide. Oxford is a registered trade mark of Oxford University Press in the UK and in certain other countries

Faster, Faster! text © Oxford University Press 2018

Edward Lear's Scrapbook text © Michaela Morgan 2014
Illustrations © Deborah Zemke 2014

History's Marvellous Mistakes text © Ciaran Murtagh 2014
Illustrations © David Semple 2014

Smoke Signals to Smartphones text © Becca Heddle 2018
Illustrations © Dan Duncan 2018

Meet a Genius text © Oxford University Press 2018
Illustrations © Alex Paterson 2018

The moral rights of the authors have been asserted

This Edition published in 2020

British Library Cataloguing in Publication Data
Data available

ISBN: 978-0-19-277387-6

10 9 8 7 6 5 4 3 2

Paper used in the production of this book is a natural, recyclable product made from wood grown in sustainable forests. The manufacturing process conforms to the environmental regulations of the country of origin.

Printed in China

Acknowledgements

Series Editor: Nikki Gamble

Faster, Faster!

The publisher would like to thank the following for permission to reproduce photographs: **p8:** 4x6/Istockphoto; **p8:** PhotoEuphoria/iStockphoto; **p8:** Blue Jean Images/Alamy Stock Photo; **p9t:** De Agostini/E.Pagni/Getty Images; **p9b:** Ed Darack/Getty Images; **p10:** DEA Picture Library/Getty Images; **p11:** Granger Historical Picture Archive/Alamy Stock Photo; **p12:** Topical Press Agency/Getty Images; **p13t:** DEA Picture Library/Getty Images; **p13m:** Maxim Petrichuk/123RF; **p14:** Flavio Vallenari/iStockphoto; **p10:** seewhatmitchsee/iStockphoto; **p14:** Marionette/stock.adobe.com; **p14:** phonlamaiphoto/stock.adobe.com; **p15t:** DEA/M. Seemuller/Getty Images; **p15b:** Bettmann/Getty Images; **p16:** Hulton Collection/Getty Images; **p17t:** Spaarnestad Photo/Mary Evans; **p17b:** Shutterstock.com; **p18:** Topical Press Agency/Getty Images; **p19t:** Hulton Archive/Getty Images; **p19b:** James W Copeland/Shutterstock.com; **p20:** Sueddeutsche Zeitung Photo/Alamy Stock Photo; **p21t:** Granger Historical Picture Archive/Alamy Stock Photo; **p22:** Stan Honda/Getty Images; **p23l:** Stocktrek Images/Getty Images; **p23r:** Edward Slater/Getty Images; **p25tl:** Monkey Business/stock. adobe.com; **p25tr:** Robert Mcgrath/Getty Images; **p27:** Stocktrek Images/ Getty Images. All other photographs by Shutterstock.

Edward Lear's Scrapbook

The publisher would like to thank the following for permission to reproduce photographs: **p32 & p33t:** Alamy/V&A Images; **p33b:** The Royal Archives/©HM Queen Elizabeth II 2012; **p34l:** Corbis/stapleton collection; **p34r:** Alamy/V&A Images; **p35l:** Shutterstock/A. Kaiser; **p35r:** The National Portrait Gallery /Edward Lear; **p36:** Wikipedia Commons (out of copyright); **p37:** Bridgeman Art Library/Edward Lear; **p38 & p39:** The Bodleian Library, University of Oxford 2014; 2529e.2; **p40t:** Shutterstock/A. Kaiser; **p40:** Alamy/V&A Images; **p41:** Topfoto/ The Grainger Collection, New York; Background images: Shutterstock/ Daniel Cozma; Shutterstock/A. Kaiser; Shutterstock/oriontrail;

History's Marvellous Mistakes

The publisher would like to thank the following for permission to reproduce photographs: **p53:** Charles J Sharp/Wiki Commons; **p54t:** Bettman/Corbis; **p54b:** Photo Researchers/Mary Evans Picture Library; **p59:** Mary Evans Picture Library/Alamy; **p60:** Bettman/Corbis; **p60-65** (background): CNRI/Science Photo Library; **p62:** Food & Drug Administration/Science Photo Library; **p65:** Steve Vidler/Alamy.

Smoke Signals to Smartphones

The publisher would like to thank the following for permission to reproduce photographs: **p70(TL):** Kali9/iStockphoto; **p70(BR):** BRIAN MITCHELL/Corbis Documentary/Getty Images; **p70(BL):** Myrleen Pearson/Alamy Stock Photo; **p72:** Jerome Chatlin/Gamma-Rapho/ Getty Images; **p74:** David Bank/Getty Images; **P75:** Ashley Cooper/ Alamy Stock Photo; **P76:** Everett Collection Historical/Alamy Stock Photo; **P78:** Nsf/Alamy Stock Photo; **P80:** Photo12/UIG/Getty Images; **P81(B):** SSPL/Getty Images; **P81(T):** Amoret Tanner/Alamy Stock Photo; **P16(TL):** Stockfolio/Alamy Stock Photo; **P82(TR):** The Print Collector/ Print Collector/Getty Images; **P84(T):** DeAgostini/Getty Images; **P84(B):** Hulton Archive/Getty Images; **P86(T):** Bettmann/Getty Images; **P86(B):** H. Armstrong Roberts/Getty Images; **P88:** WENN Ltd / Alamy Stock Photo; **P90(T):** Underwood Archives/Getty Images; **P90(B):** Science History Images/Alamy Stock Photo; **P92(T):** D. Hurst/Alamy Stock Photo; **P92(BKGD):** NASA; **P95(T):** J Marshall - Tribaleye Images/Alamy Stock Photo; All other images by Shutterstock.

Meet a Genius

The publisher would like to thank the following for permission to reproduce photographs: **p101 & p125l:** DEA/A. DAGLI ORTI/Getty Images; **p102:** The Mozart family, 1780-81 (oil on canvas), Croce, Johann Nepomuk della (1736-1819) / Mozart Museum, Salzburg, Austria / Alinari / Bridgeman Images; **p106:** Art Collection 2 / Alamy Stock Photo; **p108t:** Roland Schlager / EPA/REX/Shutterstock; **p108b:** Granger Historical Picture Archive / Alamy Stock Photo; **p109 & p125:** middle: Boyer/Getty Images; **p110:** Granger Historical Picture Archive/Alamy Stock Photo; **p114r:** Science Photo Library; **p114l:** Pictorial Press Ltd/ Alamy Stock Photo; **p116:** Boyer/Getty Images; **p117 & p125r:** Granger Historical Picture Archive/Alamy Stock Photo; **p122l:** Master and Fellows of Trinity College Cambridge; **p122r:** Master and Fellows of Trinity College Cambridge; All other images: Shutterstock & iStock.

Cover images Shutterstock